The Norwegian Christmas Cookbook

Marit Peters

Contents

Introduction

Christmas is very popular in Norway, and the snowy Nordic setting suits many Christmas traditions making it a magical time.

There are Christmas markets, parties and numerous other traditions and customs. The main day of Christmas in Norway is Christmas Eve on 24 December. A big part of these celebrations and occasions is Christmas food. There are many traditional Norwegian Christmas foods which are influenced by Norway's long history and rural nature. These include many meat dishes – some rather bizarre - and fish dishes as Norway is famous for its seafood. Norwegian Christmas cookies and desserts are also wonderful.

Try some Norwegian recipes this Christmas in this book – The Norwegian Christmas Cookbook

Fried Apples

Ingredients

7 chopped apples
100g/half a cup of brown sugar
1 teaspoon of cinnamon
half a teaspoon of cardamom
4 tablespoons of butter

Cook the apples in the butter in a pan for 5 minutes. Add the rest of the ingredients and cook on a medium heat for 15 minutes.

Serve with meat.

Redcurrant Jelly

Ingredients

900g/1.9 lb of redcurrants
800g/1.7 lb of sugar
1 tablespoon of lemon juice

Put the currants in a pan. Add 60ml of water. Bring to the boil. Mash the redcurrant lightly with a fork. Leave to cool for 6 minutes.

Put the contents into a jelly bag. Pour currants into the bag. Place over a bowl and leave to strain for 8 hours.

Put the strained liquid in a saucepan. Add the sugar and lemon juice. Cook on a medium heat until the sugar has dissolved. Boil for 10 minutes - until set.

Store in jars.

Cucumber Salad

Ingredients

2 sliced cucumbers
1 tablespoon of chopped parsley
2 tablespoons of sugar
2 tablespoons of white vinegar
caraway seeds
1 teaspoon of black pepper
1 teaspoon of salt

Mix the vinegar, salt, pepper, sugar, parsley and some caraway seeds.

Layer the cucumber in a bowl. Pour over the vinegar mix. Put a weighted down plate on top of the bowl and place in the refrigerator for 1 hour.

Mushroom Sauce

Ingredients

300g/10.5 oz of sliced mushrooms
1 tablespoon of finely chopped onion
1 tablespoon of butter
1 tablespoon of flour
230ml/1 cup of cream
2 teaspoons of soy sauce
2 tablespoons of sour cream
salt
pepper

Cook the mushrooms in butter for 8 minutes.

Add the flour and mix to make a paste like sauce. Add the cream and cook for 10 minutes on a medium heat stirring all the time.

Add some salt and pepper and the soy sauce. Add the sour cream before serving.

Serve with meat.

Butter with Tomato

Ingredients

6 tablespoons of butter
2 tablespoons of tomato puree/paste
half a teaspoon of salt
half a teaspoon of sugar

Mix the ingredients to make a smooth paste - preferably with a blender. Place in the refrigerator and serve cool. Serve with fish.

Creamed Fish Soup

Ingredients

900g/2 lb of chopped cod fillet (skinless and boneless)
2 chopped carrots
1 chopped celeriac
5 chopped new potatoes
3 chopped cloves of garlic
2 chopped stalks of celery
half a chopped onion
1 chopped leek
720ml/3 cups of fish stock
480ml/2 cups of milk
240ml/1 cup of cream
10g/half a cup of chopped dill
3 tablespoons of lemon juice
salt
pepper

Put 7 tablespoons of butter in a saucepan. Add the celery, garlic, onions and leek with some salt and pepper. Cook on a medium heat for 10 minutes.

Add the carrots, potato, celeriac, milk, cream and fish stock, Boil then cook on a medium heat for 30 minutes.

Add the fish and cook on a medium heat for 10 minutes. Add the dill, lemon juice and some more salt and pepper.

Mashed Potatoes with Cheese

Ingredients

1.7 kg/7 cups cold mashed potato
240ml/1 cup hot milk
166g/2 cups of chopped Jarlsberg cheese
olive oil
salt

Mix the potato, milk and 1 and a half cups of the cheese. Put in a greased baking dish. Put the rest of the cheese on top with some salt and a little olive oil. Cook in a medium oven for 30 minutes.

Dill Sauce

Ingredients

480ml/2 cups of sour cream
1 tablespoon of mustard
2 tablespoons of fresh dill
1 tablespoon of lemon juice
1 teaspoon of salt
half a teaspoon of pepper

Mix the ingredients on a bowl. Place in the refrigerator for 2 hours.

White Sauce

Ingredients

480ml/2 cups of milk
half a chopped onion
1 bay leaf
5 tablespoons of butter
4 tablespoons of flour
salt
pepper

Put the milk in a pan. Cook on a medium heat for 5 minutes. Add the bay leaf and onion and cook on a medium heat for 5 minutes. Drain the liquid keeping the milk and removing the bay leaf and onion.

Put the butter in a pan and melt. Add the flour and mix to make a paste. Add the milk and stir. Cook on a low heat for 10 minutes, stirring constantly.

Add some salt and pepper.

Wine Sauce

Ingredients

1 tablespoon of chives
1 chopped shallot
1 teaspoon of chopped thyme
110ml/half a cup of red wine
230ml/1 cup of fish stock
butter
salt
pepper

Fry the shallot in some butter with the chives and thyme for 6 minutes.

Add the stock and wine and cook on a low heat for 10 minutes - until sauce has reduced by half.

Strain the sauce into a bowl. Whisk in 2 tablespoons of butter. Add some salt and pepper.

Prune and Juniper Stuffing

Ingredients

250g/8.8 oz of chopped prunes (with stones take out)
2 teaspoons of crushed juniper berries
3 chopped onions
2 cloves of garlic
1 stick of chopped celery
2 chopped apples
240g/8.46g of fresh breadcrumbs
20g/0.7 oz of chopped fresh parsley
2 beaten eggs
butter

Put some butter in a pan and fry the garlic, celery and onions for 15 minutes. Remove from the heat, and add the juniper berries, apples, prunes, breadcrumbs, parsley and eggs. Add some salt and pepper and mix.

Put the mix in baking tray greased with butter. Put some parchment paper on top and cook in preheated oven at 220C/428F for 30 minutes.

Serve with turkey.

Madeira Sauce

Ingredients

3 chopped shallots
1 tablespoon of tomato paste/puree
3 tablespoons of flour
180ml/two thirds of a cup of Madeira
500ml/2 cups of chicken stock/broth
butter
2 tablespoons of soy sauce

Cook the shallots in some butter for 8 minutes. Add the flour and tomato paste. Mix to make a paste. Add the stock and Madeira and bring to the boil, whisking all the time. Add some salt and pepper and the soy sauce and cook on a low heat for 8 minutes. Stir in 2 tablespoons of butter.

Sauerkraut

Ingredients

1 chopped cabbage
1 tablespoons of caraway seeds
1 and a half tablespoons of butter
8 tablespoons of sugar
280ml/9.4 fl oz of water
8 tablespoons of apple cider vinegar

Put the cabbage, caraway seed, butter and salt in a pan. Add the water. Cook on a medium heat for 2 hours 10 minutes.

Add the vinegar and sugar.

Sandefjord Butter Sauce

Ingredients

juice from 2 lemons
110ml/half a cup of cream
4 tablespoons of butter
salt
cayenne pepper
fresh parsley

Put the lemon juice in a pan. Cook on a medium heat for 5 6 minutes. Add the cream and mix. Cook for 5 minutes. On a low heat add the butter and whisk in. Cook on a low heat for 8 minutes stirring all the time. Add some cayenne pepper, salt and chopped parsley. Mix well.

Brown Gravy

Ingredients

half a grated onion
1 tablespoon of cornstarch/cornflour
1 beef bouillon cube
1 teaspoon of sea salt
half a teaspoon of nutmeg
half a teaspoon of black pepper
3 crushed dried juniper berries
700ml/3 cups of beef stock/broth
30ml/1 fl oz of milk
30ml/1 fl oz of cream

Put the ingredients in a bowl and whisk well.

Put in a pan and stir. Bring to the boil, then cook on a low heat for 8 minutes, stirring all the time.

Strain the liquid.

Christmas Food Trivia

Many Norwegians have turkey for dinner on New Year's Eve. It is served with side dishes such as Brussels sprouts cauliflower, apples, prunes and grapes.

Breakfast is a popular dish on Christmas day. There are often several dishes eaten and the breakfast lasts for a long time. Typical dishes are leftovers from the Christmas meal eaten on Christmas Eve and dishes such as smoked salmon, brawn and scrambled eggs.

In eastern Norway pork ribs are a more popular Christmas Eve dish. In western Norway mutton ribs are more popular.

From November a Julebord is held. This is a Christmas buffet with Christmas food and drink. Companies and schools hold a Julebord during the Christmas period.

The Julebord tradition - the Christmas buffet - comes from communal parties held in medieval Norway.

At Christmastime Norwegian breweries release a Christmas beer. The beer is a dark and strong brew.

Kale with Cream

Ingredients

450g/1 lb of kale leaves
240m1/ cup of milk
240ml/1 cup of cream
salt
pepper

Put the kale in a pan with some salt. Cover with water. Cook on a medium heat for 17 minutes - until cooked.

Drain, then chop.

Put the butter in a pan and mix in the flour to make a paste. Add the milk and cream. Cook on a low heat stirring all the time to make a thick sauce.

Add some salt and pepper. Add the kale and mix.

Pork Ribs

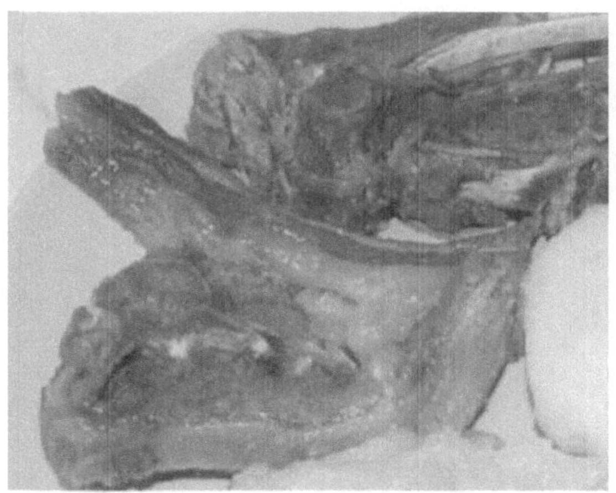

Lamb Ribs

Boiled Potatoes with Parsley

Ingredients

peeled small potatoes
chopped fresh parsley
butter
salt
pepper

Put the potatoes in a pan of salted water. Cover and bring to the boil. Cook on a medium heat for 15 minutes - until cooked.

Drain. Add parsley, butter and some salt and pepper.

Cabbage and Cream

Ingredients

340g/14 oz of chopped cabbage
2 tablespoons of butter
4 tablespoons of flour
360ml/1 and a half cups of milk
a teaspoon of chicken stock power/bouillon
salt
pepper
nutmeg

Put the cabbage in a pan of water and cook on a high heat for
30 minutes. Drain.

Mix the flour and butter in a pan to make a paste. Add the milk
and stock/bouillon and stir to make as smooth mix.

Add the cabbage to the pan with some salt, pepper and nutmeg
and mix well.

Potato Dumplings

Raspball

Ingredients

5 peeled and grated potatoes
chopped ham cubes
400g/3 cups of flour
1 egg
butter
salt
pepper

Put the potatoes in a pan with the egg, flour and some salt. Make a dough.

Form the dough into dumplings - about 12. Put a cube of ham inside each dumpling.

Put the dumplings in a pan of water on a medium heat. Cook for 50 minutes.

Drain.

Serve with melted butter and some salt and pepper.

Crispbread

Ingredients

140g/5 oz of rye flour
170g/6 oz of plain flour
40g/1.4 oz of dark rye flour
300ml/1 and a quarter cups of warm water
1 tablespoon of yeast
2 teaspoons of salt

Put the yeast and water in a bowl.

Mix the rye and plain flour. Add the salt and yeast mix. Make a dough. Knead on a board sprinkled with dark rye flour for 6 minutes. Cut into 13 pieces. Make into balls. Put the balls on a baking dish, cover with a damp towel and leave for 25 minutes,

Roll the balls out into flat shapes. Place on a greased baking tray. Cook in a preheated oven at 220C/428F for 10 minutes.

Coleslaw

Ingredients

1 shredded cabbage
2 grated carrots
150g/1 and half cups of chopped celery
1 chopped green bell pepper
1 teaspoon of celery seed
180g/6.3 oz of sugar
240ml/1 cup of white vinegar
1 tablespoon of salt

Put the cabbage in a bowl. Add the salt. Place in the refrigerator for 3 hours.

Put the vinegar in a pan with the celery seeds and sugar. Cook on allow heat for 12 minutes. Leave to cool.

Put the vegetables and bell pepper in the bowl with the cabbage. Add the vinegar mix. Place in the refrigerator for 24 hours.

Christmas Food Trivia

A Christmas soda is produced in Norway at Christmas called a julebrus.

A rice pudding - a risengrynsgrøt - is eaten on Christmas Eve.

One blanched almond is put in the rice, and whoever gets it wins a prize of a marzipan pig.

Ribbe - pork rib - is usually eaten with sausages, meatballs and sauerkraut.

Pinnekjøtt - lamb or mutton rib - is usually eaten with mashed root vegetables and potatoes.

Although there is a choice between pork rib or mutton/lamb ribs for Christmas Eve dinner, most Norwegians will eat both over the Christmas period.

One dish - popular in Fjord Norway is smalahove. This is a sheep's head.

The whole head is burnt, then smoked and finally boiled. The ears and eyes are eaten first.....

Christmas dinner is Norway is usually served between 5 and 8pm on Christmas Eve.

Waldorf Salad

Ingredients

3 peeled and chopped apples
150g/1 cup of grapes
140ml of mayonnaise
1 tablespoon of sugar
salt
1 teaspoon of lemon juice
60g/half a cup of walnuts

Mix the sugar, lemon juice, mayonnaise and some salt in a bowl. Add the rest of the ingredients and mix. Place in the refrigerator before serving.

Celeriac Puree

Ingredients

1 chopped and peeled celeriac/celery root
110ml/half a cup of milk
110ml/half a cup of water
2 tablespoons of butter
salt
pepper

Put the celeriac in a pan with the milk and water. Bring to the boil then cook on a low heat for 15 minutes - until tender

Put the celeriac and liquid in a blender and make a smooth mix.

Put in a pan and add the butter and some salt and pepper. Cook on a medium heat until thickened.

Potato Lefsa

Ingredients

12 large peeled, boiled and mashed potatoes
118ml/half a cup of cream
28g/half a cup of butter
540g/4 cups of flour
1 tablespoon of salt
1 tablespoon of sugar

Mix the mashed potatoes with the butter, cream, sugar and salt. Put in a bowl and place in the refrigerator for 10 hours.

Stir in the flour to the potatoes mix. Form into 12 balls. Roll out the balls on a floured surface.

Put the lefsa in a frying pan or skillet and cook on a high heat for two minutes on each side.

Herring with Sour Cream

Waldorf Salad

Root Vegetable Mash

Ingredients

500g/1.1 lb of peeled and chopped swede
250g/8.8 oz of peeled and chopped carrot
40g/1.14g of butter
100ml/3.3 fl oz of cream
salt
pepper

Put the swede and carrot in pan of hot water - enough to cover them. Cover and bring to the boil, then cook on a low heat for 15 minutes. Take off the heat, then cook on a high heat for another 5 minutes.

Remove the pan from the heat. Drain the water. Mash the vegetables with the butter, cream and some salt and pepper.

Liver Pate

Ingredients

800g/1.7 lb of chopped liver
450g/1 lb of chopped pork fat
4 anchovy fillets
3 eggs
113g/4 oz of chopped chicken
half a chopped onion
473ml/half a pint of cream
85g/3 oz of flour
3 teaspoons of salt
pepper

Put some of fat in a rectangular tin to line it.

In another bowl add the liver, chicken anchovies, onion and the rest of the fat. Put this mix into a blender or another mincer to make a grown/minced mix.

Mix the eggs, cream and flour to make a paste. Add to the liver mix. Add some salt and pepper.

Put the mix in the other tin. Cover with foil or parchment paper. Put in a baking dish half filled with water.

Cook in a preheated oven at 176C/350F for 1 hour 40 minutes.

Cool.

Cabbage and Bacon

Ingredients

1 chopped cabbage
10 bacon rashers
1 tablespoon of caraway seeds
50ml/1.7 fl oz of white wine vinegar
50g/1.7 oz of sugar
2 tablespoons of flour
salt
pepper

Put two slices of the bacon on the bottom of a saucepan. Add some cabbage, some flour, then sprinkle over some caraway seeds. Add some salt and pepper. Repeat the layers until all the ingredients are used up.

Add some water to fill the pan 70%. Bring to the boil, then cook on a low heat for 40 minutes - until cabbage is cooked. Add the sugar and vinegar.

Cabaret

Ingredients

180g/6 oz of cooked crab meat
180g/6 oz of cooked shrimp
40g/1.14 oz of powdered gelatine
4 sliced hard boiled eggs
2 chopped cooked asparagus stalks
1 cooked chopped carrot
1 chopped and cooked leek
2 tablespoons of fresh dill
1 litre/4 cups of fish stock

Put the gelatin in a pan with the fish stock. Bring to the boil stirring all the time.

Pout some of the gelatine in a round jelly mould or moulds. Leave to firm up. Arrange the rest of the ingredients in the mould. Pour over the rest of the gelatine to cover. Place in the refrigerator to firm up.

Trout with Sour Cream Sauce

Ingredients

4 gutted trout
240ml/1 cup of sour cream
1 teaspoon of lemon juice
butter
flour
parsley
salt
oil

Add some salt to the inside of the fish. Coat the fish in some flour.

Fry the trout in a mix of half butter and half oil for 5 minutes on each side on a medium heat. Remove the fish and any excess fat from the pan.

Put 2 tablespoons of butter in the pan. cook on a low heat for 2 minutes and stir. Add the cream and cook for 4 minutes on a low heat. Add the lemon juice. Serve over the fish and add some parsley.

Oyster Stew

Ingredients

12 oysters
480ml/2 cups of cream
480ml/2 cups of milk
1 tablespoon of butter
chopped dill
salt
pepper

Put the oysters in a pan. Cover with water. Cook on a low heat for 35 minutes.

In a separate pan put the milk, butter and cream. Cook on a low heat for 30 minutes.

Pour the milk mix over the oysters and add the dill. If you have any strained oyster juice from a jar or fresh oysters then add it. Cook on a low heat for 1 hour. Add some salt and pepper and chopped dill.

Whole Baked Salmon

Ingredients

1 whole descaled and gutted salmon
1 sliced red onion
1 sliced carrot
1 sliced lemon
chopped dill
chopped parsley
2 tablespoons of lemon juice
80g/2.8 oz of butter
extra butter
sea salt
pepper

Cut slices into salmon and put pieces of lemon, carrot, dill, parsley and red onion in them. Add some lemon juice.

Put a piece of buttered foil on a baking tray. Add some salt and pepper. Put the fish on top. Put another piece of foil on top and make a parcel.

Cook in a preheated oven at 204C/400F for 2 hours.

Remove the vegetables and skin from the fish before serving.

Christmas Food Trivia

In the south of Norway cod is a popular Christmas Eve main meal, served with Sandefjord butter sauce, carrots, and potatoes. If it is not eaten on Christmas Eve it is eaten over the Christmas period.

Lutefisk is a traditional Scandinavian Christmas dish which is fermented fish treated with lye. It was first eaten in Norway in the 15th Century.

Rakfisk is a fermented fish dish with a freshwater fish such as trout.

It is coated with salt and sugar and left for several months. It is served as an appetizer with onions and sour cream.

Clementines and nuts are a traditional part of the Norwegian Christmas.

The two most popular alcoholic drinks for Norwegians at Christmas are beer and aquavit.

The Norwegian version of mulled wine - Gløgg - is served at Christmas.

A children's version is made using fruit juice instead of wine.

Salt and Sugar Cured Cod

Persetorsk

Ingredients

300g/10 oz of cod fillets with skin on
80g/2.8 oz of salt
80g/2.8 oz of sugar
230g/8.11 oz of butter

Coat the skinless side of the fillets with sugar and salt. Place in a dish. Put something on top of the fish such as a saucepan. Leave in the refrigerator for 4 hours.

Rinse the fish. Cook in a preheated oven at 200C/392F for 8 minutes.

Herring with Sour Cream

Ingredients

283g/10 oz of chopped pickled herring fillets
1 chopped onion
1 tablespoon of chopped dill
240m/1 cup of sour cream
pepper

Mix the onion, sour cream, dill and some pepper. Add the herring. Place in the refrigerator for 2 hours.

Ground Fish

Ingredients

900g/2 lbs haddock with skin and bone removed
2 tablespoons of corn flour
1 litre/2 pints milk
2 tablespoons of salt

Mince/grind the fish. put in a bowl. Gradually add the milk, salt and flour and mix.

Shape the fish into balls. Put in a pot of boiling lightly salted water, then cook on allow heat for 3 minutes.

Christmas Cod

Ingredients

1 kg/2.2 lb of cod fillet
1 tablespoon of chopped fresh ginger
2 star aniseed cloves
1 bay leaves
4 black peppercorns
2 tablespoons of sea salt
100ml/3.3 fl oz of olive oil

Put some salt on the cod fillets. Put the fish in a bowl of cold water for 4 minutes. Drain.

Put the olive oil, peppercorns, salt, aniseed and ginger in a baking dish. Put the fish on top. Cook in a preheated oven at

Pork Ribs

Ribbe

Ingredients

500g/1.5 kg pork rib
2 and a half tablespoons of salt
2 teaspoons of pepper
water

Rub the rib with salt and pepper. Cover with foil and place in the refrigerator for 2 days.

Put the rib on a roasting dish. Add 230ml/1 cup of water and cover the meat with tin foil. Cook in a preheated oven at 240C/464F for 40 minutes. Remove foil and cook at 210C/410F for 2 hours.

Roast Beef and Juniper Berries

Ingredients

1 beef sirloin roast
1 chopped onion
3 chopped cloves of garlic
1 tablespoon of lemon zest
14 juniper berries
7 black peppercorns
3 tablespoons of thyme
sprigs of thyme
1 teaspoon of sea salt

Mix the juniper berries, peppercorns, lemon zest, thyme and garlic in a bowl and crush them. Add to 3 tablespoons of olive oil. rub over the beef.

Put the onion and some thyme sprigs in a roasting pan. Put the beef on top. Leave for 1 hour.

Cook in a preheated oven at 428F.220C for 30 minutes. Then cook at 180C/356F for 1 hour.

Leave to rest for 25 minutes before carving.

Mutton Roll

Ingredients

1 flank/skirt of mutton
chopped pork
finely chopped onion
chopped parsley
dried ginger powder
salt
pepper

Rub some salt, pepper and ginger one side of the meat. Add the onion, parsley and pork pieces one half of the meat. Roll the meat and tie with string.

Put in a heavy pot such as a Dutch oven. Cover the meat with water. Bring to the boil. Cook on a low heat for 2 hours.

Remove the meat and put on a plate. Put a plate on top and something heavy such as a brick on top to squeeze out excess moisture from the meat. Leave for 2 hours. Remove the string from the meat and slice thinly.

Roast Goose

Ingredients

1 goose
900g/2 lb of peeled and chopped apple (apple such as granny smith or bramley)
450g/1 lb of destoned prunes
227g/1 cup of butter
sea salt

Rub the inside of the goose with some sea salt.

Mix the apple and prunes/ Stuff the goose with the mix. Tie up the goose.

Mix the butter with a little water.

Put the goose on a rack in a roasting pan. Cook in a preheated oven at 226/440F for 35 minutes. Drain the fat. Cook the goose for 2 hours basting regularly with the butter mix. Turn the goose over several times during cooking.

Christmas Food Trivia

A Christmas Day (24 December) lunch - Første Juledags Frokost - is eaten.

This buffet includes such dishes as cured leg of lamb, head cheese, ox tongue, smoked salmon, pickled herring, pickled pigs trotters, ham, cheeses, jams, and various pastries and bread.

Each year Norway sends a Christmas tree to be placed in Trafalgar Square in London. This is to show gratitude for Britain supporting Norway during World War 2.

The tree is chopped down in the forest outside Oslo and a Norway spruce over 20 metres is chosen. A ceremony attended by politicians and the British ambassador to Norway is held during the chopping down of the tree.

During December Christmas markets are held in Norway with crafts, artworks, farmers produce and lots of food and drink such as mulled wine, meat dishes such as reindeer burgers and biscuits and pastries. Gingerbread houses are a popular attraction.

Marzipan Christmas treats are popular and it is said that Norway's five million population eats over 40 million marzipan Christmas sweets during the period.

Roast Turkey

Ingredients

1 turkey
duck fat

stuffing

chopped red onion
figs
cranberries
prunes
apricots
chopped apples
chopped pears
sugar
salt
lemon juice

For the stuffing, cook the apple, pear and onion in some butter and some lemon juice, salt and sugar for 6 minutes - brown them.

Add to the figs, cranberries, prunes and apricots and mix well. Stuff the turkey with the mix. The stuffing can also be cooked separately

Put some duck fat under the skin of the turkey and rub the outside with butter.

Roast the turkey for 3 hours at 190C/374F.

Pork Meat Balls

Medisterpølser

Ingredients

1 kg/2.2 lb of minced/ground pork
250g/8.8 oz of finely chopped bacon
40g/1.41 oz of potato flour or potato starch
1 teaspoon of dried ginger
300ml/10 fl oz of chicken stock
2 teaspoons of salt
1 teaspoon of black pepper

Add the pepper, ginger, meat and salt to a bowl. Mix in the stock. Add the potato flour. Roll into balls. Place in a pan of boiling water and cook on a low heat for 16 minutes.

Finish the meatballs by frying them in some oil for 5 minutes to brown them.

Pinnekjøtt

Pinnekjøtt are salted lamb ribs. Before cooking the ribs have to be soaked in water to remove the salt.

Ingredients

2 kg/4.4 lb of pinnekjøtt lamb ribs

Put the ribs in a bowl of water. Leave - at room temperature - for 35 hours.

Put a metal rack in a casserole pot. - or prepared birch sticks. Add water up to the level of the rack. Put the lamb on top. Cover and cook on a low heat for 3 hours.

Pork with Prunes

Ingredients

1 pork loin
250g/9 oz of destoned prunes
allspice powder
salt
pepper

Put the prunes in hot water for 15 minutes.

Rub the meat with allspice, salt and pepper. Put the prunes on top. Roll the pork and tie with string.

Brown the meat in some oil in a pan on all sides. Put in a preheated oven at 204C/400F and cook for 2 hours and 10 minutes.

Christmas Ham

Ingredients

1 cooked ham
3 tablespoons of mustard
1 egg yolk
1 tablespoon of brown sugar
1 tablespoon of potato flour
2 tablespoons of cornmeal
cloves

Mix the mustard, sugar, potato flour and egg yolk. Score the top of the ham. Coat the top with the sugar mix.   Put cloves in the ham. Sprinkle over the cornmeal.

Place in a preheated oven and cook at 200C/392F for 20 minutes.

Pickled Pork

Ingredients

1.81kg/4 lb pork shoulder joint
1 chopped onion
396g/14 oz of button mushrooms
1 tablespoon of redcurrant jelly
700ml/1 and a half pints of white wine
240ml/half a cup of white wine vinegar
360ml/1 and a half cups of beef stock
120g/half a cup of sour cream
1 tablespoon of cornstarch
1 tablespoon of sugar
5 cloves
5 allspice cloves
oil

Mix the wine, vinegar, sugar, cloves, onion and some oil in a bowl and mix.

Put the pork in a bowl. Add the wine mix. Cover, then place in the refrigerator for 3 days.

Put the meat in a casserole dish with some of the marinade. Cover then cook in a preheated oven at 204C/400F for 3 hours.

Put the meat on a plate. Strain the liquid from the casserole dish and put in a pan. Add the stock, sour cream and cornstarch and mix well. Cook on a medium heat stirring all the time until the sauce has thickened. Add the redcurrant jelly and cook on a low heat for another 5 minutes.

Fry the mushrooms in some butter until cooked. Serve with the meat and sauce.

Fattigman Cookies

Ingredients

6 egg yolks
1 teaspoon of ground cardamom
100g/half a cup of sugar
120g/half a cup of whipped cream
1 tablespoon of brandy
230g/2 cups of flour
half a teaspoon of salt
1 teaspoon of baking powder
120g/half a cup of meted butter

Mix the sugar and egg yolks to make a paste. Add the cream and brandy and mix.

In another separate bowl mix the cardamom, flour, baking powder and salt. Add to the other mix. Add the melted butter and make a dough. Place in the refrigerator for 10 hours.

Roll out the dough. Cut out the cookies using a fattigman cutter. Alternatively the shapes can be cut into cookie sized diamond shapes suing a knife or pizza slicer.

Fry in oil until golden. Dust with powdered sugar.

Spice Cookies

Sirupsnipper

Ingredients

158ml/ two thirds of a cup of cream
70g/2.4 oz of treacle
70g/2.4 oz of sugar
50g/1.7 oz of butter
220g/7.7 oz of flour
half a teaspoon of pepper
pinch of ground ginger
pinch of ground star anise
pinch of ground cinnamon
half a teaspoon of salt
half a teaspoon of baking soda
50g/1.7 oz of almonds
1 egg white

Put the treacle, sugar and cream in a pan. Bring to the boil and cook for 5 minutes.

Remove from the heat. Add the butter and baking soda and mix. Cool.

Add the flour, pepper, ginger and cinnamon to the treacle mix. Make a dough.

Place in plastic wrap and place in the refrigerator for 24 hours.

Roll out the doll. Cut out cookie shapes. Brush with egg white and top each cookie with an almond. Cook in a preheated oven at 180C/356F for 20 minutes.

Rice Pudding

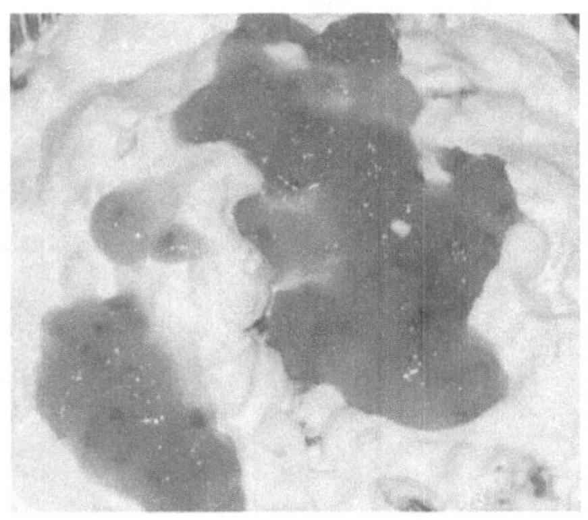

Cloudberry Cream

Caramel Pudding

Ingredients

raspberries
130g/4.6 oz of sugar
4 eggs
1 teaspoon of vanilla seeds
400ml/13 fl oz of milk
whipped cream

Put half a cup of sugar in a saucepan. Cook on a medium heat for 6 minutes until it browns (do not burn). Take off the heat.

In another pan mix the milk and 1 tablespoon of sugar. Bring to the boil then pour into a bread tin. Leave to cool.

Mix the eggs and vanilla in a bowl. Add the milk mix and whisk. Put into the bread tin. Place the bread tin in a roasting dish with enough water to cover half the tin. Cook in a preheated oven at 250C/482F for 2 hours and 40 minutes.

Leave the pudding to cool in the tin, then place the tin in a the refrigerator for 10 hours. Take the pudding out of the tin whole before serving.

Christmas Food Trivia

A popular Christmas treat is burnt almonds.

Norwegians buy glazed apples from Christmas markets to eat at home.

In Norway December 23 is a Little Christmas Eve with one small present being opened by children.

On Christmas Eve many Norwegian families watch two fairy tale films - the Czech film Three Wishes for Cinderella (with a Norwegian voiceover) and a 1976 Norwegian film called Reisen til Julestjernen (Journey to the Christmas Star)

In Norway there are special Advent television shows with an episode everyday between 1 and 24th December. The shows are of different genres, such as children's, reality or horror.

In Norway heart shaped paper baskets called Julekurver are filled with treats and Norwegian flags and hung on the Christmas tree.

Most Norwegians decorate their Christmas tree on December 23.

In Norway Christmas gifts are distributed by Julenissen, a short bearded creature.

Krumkake

Ingredients

136g/1 cup of flour
1 egg
1 teaspoon of baking powder
half a teaspoon of salt
1 teaspoon of vanilla extract
230ml/1 cup of whipped cream
100g/half a cup of sugar
1 teaspoon of melted butter

Whisk the egg, then add to the vanilla and sugar to make a paste. Add the cream, melted butter, flour and baking powder. Make a smooth mix.

Heat a krumkake iron. Add some of the batter to the iron and cook for 1 minutes - until browned. Roll up the krumkake on a stick to make a tube shape and leave to cool.

If a krumkake iron is not available, then use a frying pan with a cake dish on top of the batter.

Almond Cookies

Ingredients

260g/2 cups of flour
400g/2 cups of sugar
225g/half a lb of butter (unsalted)
46g/half a cup of chopped almonds
1 and a half teaspoons of baker's ammonia/ammonium bicarbonate

Mix the sugar and butter to make a paste. Add the ammonia and almonds. Make into a dough. Form into 20 balls and freeze for 1 hour.

Place the cookies on a baking tray and cook in a preheated oven at 148C/300F for 35 minutes.

Gingerbread

Pepperkakke

Ingredients

160g/5.6 oz of butter
160g/5.6 oz of caster sugar
110g/3.3 oz of treacle
90g/3.17 oz of golden syrup
80ml/2.7 fl oz of milk
1 egg yolk
500g/1.1 lb of flour
2 teaspoons of ginger
2 teaspoons of cinnamon
1 teaspoon of sodium bicarbonate
half a teaspoon of black pepper
1 teaspoon of cardamom powder

Mix the sugar and butter and make a paste. add the rest of the ingredients to make a dough. Divide the mix in two, wrap in clingfilm and place in the refrigerate for 10 hours.

Roll out the dough. Cut into gingerbread man shapes or the shape or your choice. Place on a baking sheet and cook in a preheated oven (on the middle shelf of the oven) at 170C/338F for 10 minutes. Once cooled they can be decorated with icing sugar, dried fruit and sweets.

Butter Cookies

Ingredients

136g/1 cup of flour
70g/1 third of a cup of sugar
2 hard boiled egg yolks
1 teaspoon of vanilla extract
70g/1 third of a cup of butter

Mix the butter and egg yolk. Add the vanilla, sugar and flour. Make a smooth dough. Shape into cookie shapes. Place on a greased baking tray and cook in a preheated oven at 190C/375F for 15 minutes.

Queen Maud Pudding

Ingredients

80g/2.8 oz of grated dark chocolate
3 eggs
260ml/1 cup of whipped whipping/heavy cream
2 tablespoons of sugar
3 gelatin sheets

Melt the gelatin by soaking it in cold water for 15 minutes, then place in a bowl and put over a pan of boiling water until gelatin has melted.

Whisk the eggs and sugar in a bowl to make a smooth mix. Add the gelatin. Add the cream.

Put some of the mix in a bowl, followed by a layer of chocolate. Repeat the layers.

Prince's Cake

Ingredients

160g/5.6 oz of finely chopped almonds
280g/2 cups of flour
1 teaspoon of baking powder
200g/7 oz cup of sugar
150g/5.2 oz cup of butter
1 egg
140g/5 oz of powdered sugar
2 egg whites

Mix the flour, sugar and baking powder. Add the butter and create a breadcrumb type mix. Add the egg and make a dough.

Put dough in some plastic wrap and place in the refrigerator for 1 hour.

Mix the almonds, powdered sugar and egg whites to make a dough. Wrap this mix in plastic wrap and place in the refrigerator for 1 hour.

Out half the dough in a cake tin. Spread the almond mix on top. Roll out the rest of the dough and cut into strips. Place the strips on top in a lattice pattern.

Cook in a preheated oven at 190C/375F for 30 minutes.

Rice Pudding

Risengrynsgrøt

Ingredients

260g/9 oz of rice
430ml/14 fl oz of water
1 litre/4 cups of milk
butter
1 teaspoon of salt
sugar
cinnamon

Put the rice in a pan with the water and salt. Bring to the boil, then reduce heat, cover, then cook on a low heat for 13 minutes. Add the milk and bring to the boil. Cover and cook on a low heat for 30 minutes. Serve with sugar, cinnamon and butter on top.

Cloudberry Cream

Ingredients

600g/1.3 lb of cloudberry jam or fresh cloudberries
7 tablespoons of sugar
700ml/3 cups of cream
1 vanilla bean
3 teaspoons of chopped fresh lavender

Put the cream and sugar in a bowl. Add the vanilla seeds.
Whip the cream. Add the jam and lavender and mix gently.

Smultringer

Ingredients

4 egg yolks
280g/10 oz of sugar
2 egg whites
85g/3 oz of melted butter
1 teaspoon of cardamom powder
450g/1 lb of flour
120ml/a quarter of a pint of heavy cream
half a teaspoon of Ammonium bicarbonate (hartshorn salt)
vegetable oil

Mix the eggs, cream, sugar, flour, cardamom, butter and ammonium bicarbonate to make a smooth mix. Place in the refrigerator for 24 hours.

Make into long thin strips. Make the strips into rings.

Fry in hot fat until they have browned.

Goro Cookies

Ingredients

250g/9 oz of butter
200g/1 cup of sugar
2 eggs
180ml/three quarters of a cup of whipping cream
260g/2 cups of flour
1 teaspoon of vanilla extract

Mix the ingredients in a bowl with a whisk and make a batter.

Put 2 teaspoon of the batter on a goro iron. If a goro iron is not available use a krumkake iron, or put the batter on a griddle and use another metal object to press down on top. Cook each cookie for about a minute.

Place them on a rack to cool.

Christmas Bread

Ingredients

90g/half a cup of raisins
1 tablespoons of chopped lemon peel
100g/half a cup of sugar
half a teaspoon of salt
half a teaspoon of ground cardamom
1 teaspoon of dried yeast
1 beaten egg
2 tablespoons of butter
550g/4 cups of flour
egg white

Mix the sugar, salt, cardamom and milk. Add the yeast and leave for 10 minutes.

Add the butter, egg, raisins, lemon peel and flour and mix. Make a dough and knead for 5 minutes.

Leave to rise in a warm place for 1 hour.

Make into a bread loaf shape and place in a bowl. Cover with plastic wrap then leave for 1 hour to double in size.

Brush with egg white. Cook in a preheated oven at 176C/350F for 40 minutes.

Apple Porridge

Ingredients

800g/1.76 lb of peeled and chopped apples
1 teaspoon of ground cardamom
90g/3.17 oz of brown sugar
1 and a half tablespoons of lemon juice
240ml/1 cup of water

Put all the ingredients in a pan. Cover, then boil. Cook on a low heat for 30 minutes.

Put through a sieve or in blender to create a smooth mix.

Serve with whipped cream.

Gløgg

Mulled Wine

Ingredients

750ml/2 and a quarter cups of red wine
1 stick of cinnamon
1 tablespoon of chopped ginger
1 tablespoon of chopped dried orange peel
8 cloves
5 cardamom pods
85g/3 oz of sugar
almonds raisins
400ml/one and two thirds of a cup of aquavit

Put the wine in a pan. Add the cinnamon, ginger, orange, cloves, cardamom, raisins and sugar. Cook on a medium heat until the sugar has dissolved. Remove from the heat. Leave for 1 hour.

Strain the liquid into a bowl. Before serving, reheat with the aquavit. Serve in a punchbowl. Add raisins and almonds to glasses in the cups with the mulled wine.